LETS GO!

Stefanie Simon

Copyright © 2014 by Stefanie Simon.

All Rights Reserved. No part of this book may be copied or reproduced by any means, electronic or mechanical, including photocopying, recording, or any information storage and retrieval system, without prior permission in writing by the copyright owner.

LETS GO! Leaders are Emotionally mature, Thoughtful, Smart, Goal-oriented, One-on-one practitioners.™

Cover design: Anita Jovanovic
Interior page design: Megan McCullough
Editors: Jeannie Ingraham and Deborah Natelson

First printing, 2014

It never ceases to amaze me how richly God has blessed me. He started by giving me an awesome Mom and Dad, then the coolest brother, Salem, and two fabulous sisters, Suzanne and Sabrina.

And the blessings have continued throughout my life in the form of so many people who have loved me and helped me along my life's journey. Because there is simply not enough room in this book to acknowledge and thank all of them, I will name them by group: family, friends, colleagues, participants who attended a presentation or learning event I facilitated, and casual acquaintances in my daily comings and goings.

And last, but certainly not least, I want to acknowledge the amazingly talented creative team who helped me birth LETS GO!: Jeannie Ingraham and Deborah Natelson, editors; Megan McCullough, book designer; Anita Jovanovic, cover designer and illustrator; and Sarah Awa, proofreader.

I am the product of so much love and support and encouragement.

Thank you!

Table of Contents

Introduction 1

Chapter 1: **L**eaders are **E**motionally Mature 7

Chapter 2: **T**houghtful 31

Chapter 3: **S**mart 51

Chapter 4: **G**oal Oriented 67

Chapter 5: **O**ne-on-One Practitioner 83

Chapter 6: **LETS GO**! 105

Conclusion 115

"I'm looking for someone who works hard even though I'm always rude, obnoxious and angry. You'd be surprised how hard it is to find good help these days."

Introduction

Justice Sage peered over his bifocals to survey the courtroom gallery of employees. The defendants standing before him sweated profusely as he read: "You are charged with being **E**motionally immature, **T**houghtless, without business **S**marts, **G**oal-less, and neglectful of **O**ne-on-one meetings. How do you plead?"

If it were up to you, would there be a court for not-so-good leaders? Could leaders also take not-so-good employees to court? What decision would the justice and jury make? What would make leaders and employees win their case?

    The answer to that last one is easy: put the leaders (and employees) in a LETS GO! state of mind.

Leaders are Emotionally Mature, Thoughtful, Smart, Goal-oriented, One-on-one practitioners

Are you ready to learn the meaning behind LETS GO! and become a better leader?

If you've ever imagined a world where all **L**eaders are **E**motionally mature, **T**houghtful, **S**mart, **G**oal-oriented, and **O**ne-on-one practitioners who make sure their employees are happy and well-trained, then the LETS GO! philosophy is for you!

This book aims to teach you all of the parts of the LETS GO! framework so that you can implement them in your own leadership role and reap the benefits of a more productive workspace—one that boasts results without collateral damage.

I developed the LETS GO! framework to help people who lead other people improve their leadership state-of-mind and skills. My inspiration is drawn from Dr. Seuss, who taught me that complicated things can be conveyed in deceptively simple ways using illustrative examples grounded in characters.

Since we live in a world where I often hear about people who aren't hitting home runs with their teams and are instead trapped in cycles of neglect and inefficiency, I want to keep everyone positive from the start, and here again I borrow from Dr. Seuss:

> So be sure when you step,
> Step with care and great tact.
> And remember that life's
> A Great Balancing Act.
> And will you succeed?
> Yes! You will, indeed!
> (98 and ¾ percent guaranteed.)

The problems I often hear about do not stem from the idea that those in leadership positions are incapable. Instead, they indicate that they are missing one key ingredient that we should give them to provide them with proper frameworks to manage and lead.

If life is a great balancing act, then you should be balancing the different components (**E**motional maturity, **T**houghtfulness, **S**martness, **G**oal-orientation, **O**ne-on-one practices) of the LETS GO! philosophy—to have the key ingredients to success.

So who am I? What gives me the right to have developed this framework and present it before you as the solution that you need?

I am a woman who has embarked on her own journey (with many side trips) to success.

***L**eaders are **E**motionally Mature, **T**houghtful, **S**mart, **G**oal-oriented, **O**ne-on-one practitioners*

My career journey began when I graduated from college and started leading people—though I must use the term "leading" loosely here, because I was not emotionally mature enough then to lead anyone effectively. Hindsight is truly 20/20, and my past experiences have allowed me to grow and learn over time.

For more than 20 years, I have been leading people, every year a bit better than the year before. The 80/20 rule applies to my life: 80% of the time I did a great job on 20% of the most important things. I achieved success because I was deliberate and intentional about being **E**motionally mature, **T**houghtful, **S**mart, **G**oal-oriented, and a **O**ne-on-one practitioner. How I wish I'd had the LETS GO! framework at the start of my journey, before I struggled to learn how to build, develop and manage winning teams! It was only after I succeeded in developing LETS GO! that I became truly successful. And it is my hope that you can use it to become successful too!

To give you a better idea of my credentials, I offer you my personal work history. For my first job, I was a first-line supervisor for a telecommunications giant in the technology unit of their disbursement accounting department. From there, I moved on to one of the major accounting consulting firms in their Enterprise

Introduction

Resource Planning (ERP) & Business Process Re-engineering (BRP) line of business as a director. At the next stop on my journey, I served as the Vice President of Software Development for a company that developed HR, payroll, and financial software. While I was still trying to figure out what I wanted to be when I grew up (because aren't we all constantly growing up and changing?), I tried a few other organizations and even owned my own consulting/executive coaching business. I also had a brief stint in the public sector.

So my experiences are varied, and now that I have collected all them together, I want to share the result with you.

I know there are several awesome books out there on how to manage and lead, but I have always preferred something simple and practical that is easy to commit to memory. My experience tells me that leadership starts with emotional maturity, which is a dish that requires patience. Patience is the dish's first and last ingredient—and the instructions say one should fold in more patience as needed for the right consistency.

Consider this book a delectable buffet at which you are invited to sample everything and then stew over what you really liked. If you take away a tip, tool, or reminder that makes you a

***L**eaders are **E**motionally **M**ature, **T**houghtful, **S**mart,
Goal-oriented, **O**ne-on-one practitioners*

better leader, then our pool of future leaders will be better off—because you will be there to influence them!

Achieving results is ultimately all about baking yourself to perfection. So, LETS GO! lead!

Chapter 1: Leaders are Emotionally Mature

"Youth ends when egotism does; maturity begins when one lives for others."

– Hermann Hesse, *German-Swiss poet, novelist, painter, and winner of Nobel Prize in Literature*

"Now let's discuss how you treated me all those years before I was promoted to your manager."

*Leaders are **E**motionally Mature, **T**houghtful, **S**mart, **G**oal-oriented, **O**ne-on-one practitioners*

 Is it reasonable to expect our leaders to be **P**atient, **A**lert, **T**rustworthy, **I**ntentional, **E**mpathetic, and **N**ice but **T**ough?

Many people find themselves drawn to being a leader for the title and the benefits (both monetary and non-monetary) without realizing the extent of the responsibilities that go along with those benefits. Leaders must always first be emotionally mature, and that begins with looking deeply inward and asking a couple of key questions:

Do I Really Want to Do this?

It might sound like a silly question, but honestly, go ahead and ask yourself. If you can't immediately respond with an honest, heartfelt "yes," then leading may not be for you. And that's okay. That's important to know.

If you do respond with a heartfelt yes, then keep reminding yourself of that yes—every day, if you have to. Reaffirming your desire to be a great leader can only help you.

Chapter 1: Leaders are Emotionally Mature

Do I Have the Resilience to Deal with Less-Than-Ideal Employees and Organizations?

It's easy to lead employees who both want to work and can do the work. But what about those employees who do not fulfil one of those areas?

Maybe you've got an employee who can do the work but just doesn't want to. Do you have the patience and energy for that?

Or maybe you have an employee who can't do the work but earnestly wants to. Do you have the patience and energy for that?

How about less-than-ideal organizations? I don't know how many times I've heard the following or a flavor of the following: Our leaders and employees are not held accountable for their actions. They do whatever they want without consequences, and their results are often accompanied by disgruntled employees and irate customers.

Knowing how to function in less than ideal organizations and how to motivate and develop your employees through both formal and informal learning events is key. So if you feel confident in your ability to lead with patience and energy, then you're already halfway there. I'll show you just how to help unmotivated or unskilled employees in Chapters 4 and 5, "Goal-Oriented" and "One-on-One Practitioners."

Hopefully, you've answered both of the above questions positively and with an open mind about how to proceed in order to improve.

Everything ultimately comes down to people getting things done. It goes without saying (but I will) that everyone wins when a company gets things done by being good to its employees and the communities it serves—and, of course, by being efficiently profitable and relevant to their customers. Given today's accessibility of information, the overwhelming majority of companies have access to the same systems, tools, processes, policies, procedures, job roles, and organizational structures. Despite this, these companies don't all perform the same way. That's because of the people making up each company. Every individual makes a difference, and positive differences start with having emotionally mature leaders at the top.

Leadership involves building teams and developing people, which means cultivating healthy relationships. And guess what? Healthy relationships are not possible unless you as the leader are committed to being emotionally mature. This might sound like a lot to take in, but

Chapter 1: Leaders are Emotionally Mature

I'm going to break it down for you, because everything is better in pieces!

Emotionally mature leaders must be PATIENT (patient, alert, trustworthy, intentional, empathetic, and nice yet tough).

Patient

- "Patience is not simply the ability to wait—it's how we behave while we're waiting." – Joyce Meyer
- "Patience and perseverance have a magical effect before which difficulties disappear and obstacles vanish." – John Quincy Adams

We're likely all familiar with the phrase "patience is a virtue." People continue to perpetuate the phrase, deeply embedding it in our minds. I suspect that parents most often say it to their children (I know my mother and father have said it to me a great many times).

But is it really a virtue? Well, of course it is! Why else would it be on my list?

It is essentially impossible to become emotionally mature and still be an impatient person. Dealing with people on a day-to-day basis, as you do as a leader, requires patience.

Leaders are Emotionally Mature, Thoughtful, Smart, Goal-oriented, One-on-one practitioners

Impatience breeds discontent and leads to increased feelings of stress and pressure.

Imagine this: an employee is struggling to learn how to execute a specific task well. What effect does being impatient have? It likely means that you're angry and dissatisfied with the employee. That will, in turn, make that employee angry and dissatisfied, because your impatience will be evident to him or her and will likely manifest in your interactions. Because of these bad feelings, that employee will be less likely to ever learn how to execute the task at hand.

Now imagine that situation if it were handled with patience: you remain calm and understanding about this employee's struggles. This leads you to engage in meaningful conversations with him or her about how you can help him or her master this task. This in turn makes the employee feel valued and believe that you, as a leader, actually care. Caring is important. Positive feelings will make the employee more likely to master the task quickly and continue working for you with a positive and optimistic outlook.

Success can be yours. It just takes a touch of patience!

Chapter 1: Leaders are Emotionally Mature

Alert

The Merriam-Webster dictionary defines the quality of being alert as "able to think clearly and to notice things." Emotionally mature leaders need to apply that alertness: think clearly and notice things both about yourself and about others. You should be alert so that you can get along better with your colleagues, and so you can understand how other people learn and process information.

Here, it's important to remember that every person is different. You'll have your own preferences, and every employee of yours will have his or her own preferences. These preferences may intersect at certain points and may be wildly different at other points. That's part of what makes people interesting—that they're not all the same!

What kinds of things should you notice? A person's communication style, interests, beliefs, values, strengths, and challenges. While I believe in keeping things simple, you may want to delve into this topic in detail by checking out http://www.everythingdisc.com, http://www.myersbriggs.org/, or https://www.gallupstrengthscenter.com.

*Leaders are **E**motionally Mature, **T**houghtful, **S**mart, **G**oal-oriented, **O**ne-on-one practitioners*

"Whatever the circumstances of your life, the understanding of type can make your perceptions clearer, your judgments sounder, and your life closer to your heart's desire."

– Isabel Briggs Myers, *Psychologist*

Being aware of people, their personalities and preferences, is important. For example, say you've got an employee; we'll call her Sarah. You, as the leader, notice that Sarah rarely stops to take a breath. She prefers a quick reference guide to a detailed manual. Sarah also relishes sharing her thoughts with the nearest warm body. You have also observed that Sam, another member of your team, prefers the peace and quiet of independent thought and work. You have a project that will benefit from both Sarah's and Sam's strengths. Noticing their preferences ensures that you create a project environment that reduces the fuel that may lead to resistance or conflict because of their differences, maximizes their strengths, and increases the probability of project success.

Keeping a mental, virtual, or even physical file of your employees' preferences can only help you be a better leader. Plus, employees will likely really appreciate that you remember these details about them.

Chapter 1: Leaders are Emotionally Mature

This idea applies to both the individual level, as illustrated in the above example, and the collective level. Each group of people will have a unique dynamic and understanding, and being aware of that dynamic can make groups easier to run and more productive.

In addition to knowing your employees' preferences, of course, you'll need to be aware of your own preferences. If your preferences are interfering with someone else's, that could cause conflict, and you might be forced to evaluate if there's a way to find compromise or if someone (including you) needs to budge.

But the key is to be alert. Notice things! Act accordingly! Otherwise, you are liable to encounter disgruntled employees and be disgruntled yourself without knowing why. Being alert is one element that helps you be emotionally mature and a capable leader equipped with the right knowledge.

Trustworthy

According to the Merriam-Webster dictionary, being trustworthy means being able to be relied on to do or provide what is needed or right. For me, this means combining the traits of reliability, responsibility, and resilience into one.

*Leaders are Emotionally Mature, Thoughtful, Smart,
Goal-oriented, One-on-one practitioners*

Being trustworthy closely relates to the idea of setting the example that you want followed. I can guarantee that if you want your employees to be trustworthy, then you need to be so yourself! Everything starts from the top and moves down from there. If you're making a sincere effort to remain trustworthy, then your employees will be more likely to make an effort to remain trustworthy as well.

Say you've got a meeting to attend with some key employees. The responsible and reliable thing to do is to come to the meeting on time and fully prepared, with whatever materials you might need. Taking the concept a step further, this means attending the meeting at your best—making sure that you are mentally and physically prepared so that you can energize those around you.

Resilience comes into play in how you maintain your reliability and responsibility. I won't lie to you: being a leader can be taxing and exhausting. Sometimes, it's difficult to face all of the tasks you have in a day, but it's important to be resilient and to keep going no matter how challenging things are.

> 95% of the time, I count it my **joy** and pleasure to be a leader. 5% of the time, I find it challenging or I simply want to quit. I just have to remember that I love being a leader in order to keep things in perspective.

Chapter 1: Leaders are Emotionally Mature

On a day that might seem particularly hard, maybe you need to ask yourself that first question again: do I want this? Let your answer reinvigorate you so that you remain committed to being reliable and responsible to your employees!

Something important to consider is that now and again you might slip; nobody's perfect! There might be a time that you miss a meeting because of extenuating circumstances. Don't worry; it happens to everyone. What you need to ask yourself is: how can I show reliability and responsibility in the face of this absence? Consider taking the time to make an announcement or compose an email that explains why you missed the meeting and apologize for it. Being reliable and responsible is not only a matter of taking care of your tasks; it is also a matter of holding yourself accountable for any and all actions (including failures to act).

Besides, if you're honest and open with your employees, they're more likely to be honest and open with you. Transparency can only help you as you continue to prove that you are trustworthy.

Leaders are Emotionally Mature, Thoughtful, Smart, Goal-oriented, One-on-one practitioners

Intentional

As a leader, one of your goals should be to act only in intentional ways, in ways that are planned, intended, or with purpose. This requires some thought. Before you say or do something, think about your intention.

For example, Sabrina, a manager at Stuff & Co., Inc., has been passed over for a job promotion. Instead of going to her, the promotion went to her good friend, one who has worked at the company less time than Sabrina. This makes Sabrina fairly upset. The first thing she must be is aware of her feelings; she must acknowledge that she's upset. This is being alert! Once she's aware of her feelings, she should approach every interaction with her friend with intention. Sabrina should ask herself: what do I want to say to my friend and colleague? How do I want to come across?

If Sabrina completely neglects to congratulate her friend on the promotion, then she has slighted her. This is something Sabrina doesn't want. A good leader understands that not acting is as much a decision as acting. When you don't act intentionally, you act unintentionally—and create unintentional consequences.

Chapter 1: Leaders are Emotionally Mature

If, instead, Sabrina intentionally and proactively congratulates her friend on the promotion by presenting her with a card and a few words, then Sabrina has prevented an unintentional negative outcome. She has acted in an intentional way and therefore fosters goodwill between herself and her colleague.

Be intentional. Don't do things by accident; do things because you have a clear purpose and clear reasoning!

Empathetic

According to Merriam-Webster, sympathy is "the feeling you care about and are sorry about someone else's trouble, grief, misfortune, etc." Empathy is the ability to understand or even experience someone else's feelings, thoughts, or experiences. Neither means you actually have to agree with the other person's feelings, but both allow you to understand them.

In order to be an emotionally mature and effective leader, you must exercise sympathy and/or empathy. When you do so, you come to understand that every person who works for you has his or her own set of things going on in life, and any number of those things at any given time may be influencing his or her work performance. Thus, you must have empathy or sympathy when an employee asks for a few days off in order to care for his or her ailing relative.

Being able to practice a constant understanding of other people's feelings can be difficult, but it is also the most important component of being a decent human being. Without understanding, what do we have? Besides, you never know when you might need someone to show you empathy, and if you haven't ever bothered to show it, chances are, they won't either (harkening back to the Golden Rule).

Nice yet Tough

Being nice might sound a little too broad here, so I want to narrow the focus by highlighting the Merriam-Webster definition of a nice person as someone who is considerate. For our purposes, this means a person who considers the rights and feelings of other people.

At this point, things should be starting to sound a bit intertwined, because they all go together! To be properly considerate of other people's thoughts and feelings, you'll need to be patient and alert. One cannot happen without the other!

The important thing you need to remember to be nice is that you need to take the time to realize that every person you meet is going to have thoughts and feelings about any given topic or

Chapter 1: Leaders are Emotionally Mature

situation. Acknowledging your employees' thoughts and feelings about various situations is important. It makes them feel valued, lets them realize that you care, and ultimately creates a better workplace.

If you don't incorporate this step into your attempts to be emotionally mature, then it is likely that you will end up stepping on toes or offending your employees.

Remember, the key here is acknowledgement and validation! You don't have to agree with your employees' thoughts and feelings, but you do have to acknowledge them. Saying something like "I understand where you're coming from and why you feel that way" is a great step to starting a calm, helpful conversation with an employee.

Here's where the balancing act comes into play: you must be nice, but you must also be tough. According to Merriam-Webster, a tough person is both physically and emotionally strong: able to do the hard work and to deal with harsh conditions, etc. If you are too nice, you're liable to become a doormat, someone whom nobody else respects or listens to. If you are too tough, then you're liable to be viewed in a negative light and considered as someone who doesn't care about anybody else.

Leaders are Emotionally Mature, Thoughtful, Smart, Goal-oriented, One-on-one practitioners

Oh, it is a delicate balance. Sometimes leaders have to make tough decisions. It won't always be possible to please everybody and appease all preferences, and when those times come, you must be tough.

So remember, just be PATIENT: **P**atient, **A**lert, **T**rustworthy, **I**ntentional, **E**mpathetic, and **N**ice yet **T**ough.

One way to test your patience is with this list!

Now, I know being PATIENT is a lot to take in and that it's a lot to work on. Becoming patient isn't as easy as simply deciding to be patient. So be patient with yourself! Be patient as you try to incorporate these elements, as you work hard to become emotionally mature. It won't happen overnight, but it *will* happen—as long as you keep practicing being PATIENT!

Still don't believe me when I say patience is the most important element? Here are some quotes that might change your mind:
- "Have patience with all things but first of all with yourself." – Saint Francis de Sales
- "He that can have patience can have what he will." – Benjamin Franklin

Chapter 1: Leaders are Emotionally Mature

I'd like to put some of these concepts into practice by having you imagine a couple of different scenarios. In this book, I'll make use of many examples that draw from my real life experiences, but for convenience and to preserve the anonymity of those involved, I will use the fictitious company name of Stuff & Co., Inc. (They popped up earlier, and now they're here to stay.)

For this upcoming example, I would like you to think about whether or not the leader acted in an emotionally mature way:

Stuff & Co., Inc. was holding one of its regular bi-monthly meetings. During these meetings, many employees would make suggestions on how to improve on various aspects of the company. This particular day, the executive team announced that it had discussed and decided to turn a previously suggested idea into an opportunity to implement a new system and process.

Employees are often resistant to change, but one mid-level manager, Susan, was more opposed than the rest. She thought the change was stupid and proceeded to share that opinion with her team. In fact, every opportunity that she could, she blamed the new system for problems. Word spread quickly that she didn't like what was

Leaders are Emotionally Mature, Thoughtful, Smart, Goal-oriented, One-on-one practitioners

going on, and she developed a reputation for having a bad attitude and not seeking to understand the big picture.

What should Susan have done differently? How might she have reacted in an emotionally mature way even though she didn't agree with the change?

Will you agree with every decision the company you work for makes? Of course not. Below is the 4-step process that I go through whenever I don't agree with a change:

1. I ask myself, "Will the idea work?"
    a. It's hard to argue with results. If the idea will work, then who am I to oppose it? It may not be my preference, but if I sit down and honestly can't assert that it does not work, then it's time to bite my tongue.
    b. There are over a million ways of doing things, and the vast majority of those ways end up working. Say 900,000 of those ways will work. As a company, we often do not spend time discussing the 100,000 things that won't work, which means that the idea at hand likely *will* work.

Chapter 1: Leaders are Emotionally Mature

    c. So the discussion is really about preferences. Which choice, among the 900,000 feasible solutions, is the preferred choice? For example, should we use Apple products or Microsoft products? Both products work, but people can (and often have) strong (and sometimes irrational) preferences that cause the debate to rage on. So if my company chooses Apple products, but I'm a fan of Microsoft products, then I just need to sit tight and realize that Apple products will work.

2. I ask myself, "Does it violate the essence of who I am or what is important to me?"
   a. If the idea at hand does not conflict with any of my legal, moral, spiritual, or ethical beliefs, then who am I to argue with it?
3. If I pass the first two questions—if the idea will work and does not violate the essence of who I am—then I have to find a genuine and authentic way to get on board with this bright idea.
   a. I don't mean faking here, okay? I really mean genuinely and authentically getting yourself on board. How on earth do I do that?

b. First, I connect with a group of friends who also happen to be executives whom I can chat with and vent to in a safe and healthy environment. This group helps me see the big picture in an objective and rational way. If necessary, they help me get over myself.
4. This last point is optional. It occurs when I believe there is a pattern of bad ideas and that I can no longer trust my boss.
   a. If this is the case, and I'm not able to get past the first three steps of this process, then I have to ask myself the biggest of questions: do I stay despite how I feel, or do I find another job?
   b. Something we should all ask ourselves is: if things go very wrong, do I have a Plan B?

> Freedom, options, and choice are beautiful things. Many people work not because they want to, but because they have to pay the bills. Financial freedom increases your **Plan B** options. The most important thing is simply that you have a Plan B.

Chapter 1: Leaders are Emotionally Mature

If you commit yourself to following these steps, then you can react in an emotionally mature way and not like Susan over at Stuff & Co., Inc. She certainly didn't ask herself these questions, which ended up with her promoting a toxic workplace. She might not have been able to answer all of the questions successfully in order to get genuinely on board with the idea—she might even have had to leave the company if she couldn't agree. But if she felt that strongly on the matter, her leaving would have been better for all parties involved.

> My **recipe for success** only has two ingredients, and those are: 1) love God and 2) love others. This is related to the Golden Rule. It is imperative that you treat other people the way you want to be treated yourself—i.e. love them as you love yourself, but love God first.

Leaders are Emotionally Mature, Thoughtful, Smart, Goal-oriented, One-on-one practitioners

Chapter Recap

This chapter has covered a lot of valuable information, so I want to take a moment to recap the first part of the LETS GO! framework with you.

LETS GO! be **E**motionally mature leaders!

It's important to be PATIENT—**P**atient, **A**lert, **T**rustworthy, **I**ntentional, **E**mpathetic, and **N**ice yet **T**ough (the delicate balance).

Once you know the preferences of your employees, practice patience. Every person is going to be different and will require different things of you as a leader. So be patient with them. Once you think you've been patient enough, be more patient. Just keep drawing out your patience until you think there's none left, and then practice it some more.

Being emotionally mature doesn't mean that tough things will stop happening, so you need to have a good process at hand to deal with them when they do happen so that you can maintain your status as an emotionally mature leader.

I hope that my quick steps to handling situations can help you too.

Remember, ask yourself:
1. Will it work?
2. Does it violate the essence of who I am?

Chapter 1: Leaders are Emotionally Mature

If you have answered yes to the first question and no to the second question, then find a way to:

    3. Get on board with the idea while being genuine and authentic.

If tough things emerge frequently or in a pattern, ask yourself:

    4. Should I stay or go?

Chapter 2: Thoughtful

"When I step on that basketball court, I'm thinking about basketball, I'm thinking about winning – but there's so much that goes into thought about how I'm going to open this game up to others. It's so much more than just basketball."

– Carmelo Anthony, American professional basketball player

"We need to consider this new business venture carefully."

*Leaders are Emotionally Mature, Thoughtful, Smart,
Goal-oriented, One-on-one practitioners*

 Do leaders not owe it to all people in all interactions to be thoughtful? To take it upon ourselves to think things through instead of flying off the handle?

After reading Chapter 1, you know what it means to be emotionally mature. You understand how to pay attention to and consider the needs of others. Now you must also become thoughtful. But what does it mean to be thoughtful?

To be thoughtful, you must **think things through** when you are presented with situations that impact other individuals and/or you. Over the years, I have used the following steps and tips to be thoughtful. Now I present them to you:

First, think about your thinking. Sound crazy? Maybe a little, but it is absolutely necessary. Maybe a little weird at first, but then increasingly easy as you get used to it. "**Thinking** is the hardest work there is, which is probably the reason why so few engage in it." - Henry Ford, Founder of the Ford Motor Company

Second, listen.

Third, ask questions before you respond and give precise reasons for your answers.

Fourth and finally, be comfortable with the amount of time it takes—it could be a long time,

Chapter 2: Thoughtful

or it could be a short time—to work through a problem.

> If it is helpful to reference a **problem solving** model, feel free to use the following seven steps or one of the many other similar models or a hybrid thereof:
> 1) define the problem;
> 2) analyze the problem;
> 3) develop alternative solutions (are they reversible solutions?);
> 4) evaluate and compare alternative solutions;
> 5) select a solution;
> 6) execute the solution;
> 7) monitor and check the results.

Are we born thoughtful or thoughtless? Much of the way we act in life is learned behavior, and regardless of how you have learned to behave, you can always become more thoughtful. Doing so is your choice.

It should be no surprise that thoughtful leaders are more likely to yield positive results without collateral damage (such as disgruntled employees) than thoughtless leaders, making thoughtfulness a perfect component of the LETS GO! framework.

Being thoughtful requires making continually active choices on your part. You must exercise thoughtfulness at all junctures in your leadership, not merely some of the time. Consider thoughtfulness as a frame of mind that must always be active. The moment you choose not to be thoughtful, you have chosen the consequence of negative results.

*Leaders are **E**motionally Mature, **T**houghtful, **S**mart,
Goal-oriented, **O**ne-on-one practitioners*

And don't forget! All of this builds together, so we are combining your emotional maturity with thoughtfulness. Together, this combination will help you understand and be aware of your employees' individual needs and preferences (i.e. be emotionally mature), and then act on your understanding and awareness by being thoughtful (i.e. think things through) when situations arise.

I keep talking about situations that might arise. You might be thinking to yourself, what situations? Don't worry, I'm getting there. Right now, actually! I'm going to run you through a number of examples and ask you to think through them.

I'd like to start with an example in the realm of sports, because I find that it's something that many people relate to easily. It's pretty easy to picture tired and injured players who feel overworked. Go ahead and keep them in mind right now. I find that they're really similar to change-saturated employees, which many companies struggle with.

> To break down the essence of change-saturation, first we have to look at saturation. The word "saturate" is defined by Merriam-Webster as "to fill (something) completely with something." Thus someone who is nearly change-saturated is reaching the amount of change that they can handle. **Change-saturated** employees are near the limit of their ability to absorb workplace changes such as learning new systems, processes, or job responsibilities.

Example #1: Professional Sports

It's time for playoffs, and expectations are high. Everyone on the team is rising to the challenge. The players are putting in longer, harder hours to be the best they can be.

The team has a game in Los Angeles on Tuesday and a game in New York on Thursday. Dallas is the team's home. On Wednesday, a starting player gets one of those phone calls that no one wants to get. His child has been in a car accident and is in the hospital.

What do you do?

One of the first steps in asking yourself what to do in any given situation is to consider the short-term consequences and the long-term consequences.

What might some of those consequences be if you do *not* allow the player to miss the game and go home to be with his child and wife?

Short-Term Consequences
- The player will be present for the playoff games, increasing the team's likelihood of winning.
- The player will not be home to comfort his child and wife.

*Leaders are Emotionally Mature, Thoughtful, Smart,
Goal-oriented, One-on-one practitioners*

Long-Term Consequences
- The player may hold a substantial grudge against you for not allowing him to go home.
- Such a grudge could lead to disharmony on the team and disputes between you as the leader and the player.

Now, how might those consequences differ if you **do** allow the player to miss the game and go home to be by his child's bedside?

Short-Term Consequences
- The player will not be present for the playoff games, decreasing the team's likelihood of winning.
- The player will be home to take care of and comfort his child and wife.

Long-Term Consequences
- You will have earned the loyalty and gratitude of your player.
- You will carry the reputation of a caring, thoughtful leader.

These are only a few ways to think about the situation. You might also consider how the team would react to either of these decisions. Would they be pleased to know that you as their leader

Chapter 2: Thoughtful

are understanding and likely to grant such thoughtfulness to the rest of them? Would they also want him to be present to care for his child and wife? Wouldn't they consider you a fairly heartless leader if you prioritized the game over the player's emotional wellbeing?

The thoughtful choice of allowing the player to go home to take care of his child and wife may result in some undesirable short-term consequences, but it easily nets the most positive long-term consequences. And part of being a good leader is considering things long term. Beings short-sighted never helped anyone.

Example #2: Professional Sports

It is Wednesday morning. Three of your starting players played for 40 minutes yesterday in Atlanta's game. The first player got a slight ankle sprain, the second player jammed his finger, and the third player got food poisoning and is weak. All three *can* still play but have obvious setbacks.

What do you do?

Again, you want to consider the likely short-term and long-term consequences.

However, you might find yourself wanting more information for a situation, and that's reasonable! Often times, it will be possible, as the leader, to get more information. For example, you could ask each of the players if they are up to playing and if they want to. It may very well be that one of the players would prefer to power through it. Such information might change the way you should approach the situation.

While at first glance it might seem most thoughtful to tell each of the players to rest up, you are making an unfair assumption that that is what they want.

Of course, as a disclaimer, the personal safety of all people is very important and should not be dismissed, even if they themselves want you to.

For the purposes of this example and short-term and long-term consequences, you discover, by listening and asking questions, that each player would like to have the time off to rest and recover.

If you do not let the players have the requested time off, what might happen?

Short-Term Consequences
- You will have your players for the upcoming game, and, even at their less-than-best, that's better than not having them, thus improving your team's odds of winning.

Chapter 2: *Thoughtful*

- Your players will not have the time they need to recover, and thus playing may worsen their conditions.

Long-Term Consequences
- Your players will likely hold a grudge against you for forcing them to play under poor conditions.
- The likelihood of their conditions worsening means that they may have to miss other games in the future (likely more than the few games they would have missed if they'd been allowed to recover after the game in Atlanta).

If you do let the players have the requested time off, what might happen?

Short-Term Consequences
- You will not have your players for the upcoming couple of games, and they will miss practices, possibly resulting in reduced team performance.
- Your players will rest up.

Long-Term Consequences
- Your players will likely be grateful that you allowed them the time to rest up, thus currying their good favor.

*Leaders are **E**motionally Mature, **T**houghtful, **S**mart,
Goal-oriented, **O**ne-on-one practitioners*

- The opportunity to rest up should result in a speedy recovery, allowing them to get back in the game and give it 100%.

Again, you can consider how the rest of your team would view these actions to get an even better idea of how much better the thoughtful response is than the thoughtless response.

Example #3: Corporate America

Now, let's transition into examples set in the business world. Here, we return to Stuff & Co., Inc. Sabrina has worked as a manager at Stuff & Co., Inc. for five years. Stuff & Co., Inc. is currently a finalist for a multi-million dollar contract to implement an enterprise-wide solution that will support marketing, sales, operations, finance, and human resources. The stakes are high; the pressure is on.

As part of this competition, Stuff & Co., Inc. must give three one-hour presentations. The first presentation on Tuesday should provide a company overview and the proposed project strategy. The second presentation on Wednesday should describe the solution. The third presentation should discuss ongoing support and the contract.

Chapter 2: *Thoughtful*

> For this opportunity, the **project strategy** required two components: project management and change management.
>
> Project management is the process and activity of planning, organizing, motivating, and controlling resources, procedures, and protocols in order to achieve specific goals.
>
> Change management is an approach to transitioning individuals, teams, and organizations to a desired different future state.
>
> One possible desired future state would be to make sure that all employees know how to enter or update their time worked, submit if for approval, and view or print their time report.

Sabrina finds out on Monday that two of the seven-member team cannot attend—one of whom is critical for the Tuesday morning presentation. That team member, George, will not arrive in time because of flight delays. The other team member, Stella, is sick. Sabrina is thrown into disarray, and she panics. What can she possibly do? Everything is riding on these presentations, and her team members are letting her down. She wants to pull her hair out!

What would you do in Sabrina's shoes?

Again, we want to break things down by considering the likely long-term and short-term consequences of your decision.

*Leaders are Emotionally Mature, Thoughtful, Smart,
Goal-oriented, One-on-one practitioners*

First, it is important to note that requesting an adjustment to the presentation schedule was prohibited.

One response could be to have George rent a car and drive seven hours so that he makes it on time, and to tell Stella to just take some medicine and participate or be fired. Let's look at the short-term and long-term consequences for this option:

Short-Term Consequences
- Your presentation is delivered by disgruntled employees whose unhappiness is evident and reduces your odds of winning.

Long-Term Consequences
- You negatively impact employee morale and your work environment.
- Because you likely did not win, you will not achieve the annual revenue target.

Now, a different option would be for Sabrina to tell George not to worry. After all, things happen. She would tell Stella to take care of herself and get well. Sabrina would also ask her if the company could do anything to help. Let's look at the consequences of this option:

Chapter 2: Thoughtful

Short-Term Consequences
- Sabrina will be two people down for the presentations
- Sabrina could gather the team, discuss the situation, and solicit solutions to the dilemma. She could propose a few options if no viable options surface otherwise. For example, other team members or local resources could fill in. Sabrina could even fill in.

Note that the various courses that Sabrina can pursue above to mitigate any negative short-term consequences from being two team members down all reflect thoughtfulness. Also, thoughtful leaders always have a Plan B, which Sabrina has here.

If something like this happens to you, make sure you reward your team for going above and beyond and making things work despite the difficulties.

Long-Term Consequences
- Employees feel valued.
- Stella has time to recover from her illness properly.

*Leaders are Emotionally Mature, Thoughtful, Smart,
Goal-oriented, One-on-one practitioners*

- Because they feel valued, George and Stella find ways and volunteer to go above and beyond in future situations.
- The bid is likely won and the annual revenue target exceeded.

So even though things might seem grim at first for Sabrina, she realizes that she can be thoughtful towards her employees, George and Stella, be understanding of their issues, and still win the bid for Stuff & Co., Inc. It's a win-win situation across the board.

Example #4: Corporate America

During a quarterly review session, Stuff & Co., Inc. decides to partner with a company to help build their "stuff" better. Now, they have two different companies to choose from: Company A and Company B. Company A is selected by a majority vote. Executives communicate the decision to their managers, and the managers continue the line of communication by informing their associates. When Sabrina communicates the decision to her team of associates, her superstar, Bob, resists the change because he thinks Stuff & Co., Inc. should have selected Company B.

Chapter 2: Thoughtful

The partnership with Company A will begin in 90 days. What should Sabrina do? What would you do?

One option would be for Sabrina to ignore Bob and hope that his resistance will disappear with time, since he has always been a superstar employee. Let's look at the consequences of this option:

Short-Term Consequences
- Bob does not simply get over it and instead remains disgruntled over the decision.
- Bob's performance suffers because he is disgruntled.

Long-Term Consequences
- Bob's negative interaction with Company A makes the partnership more challenging than it needs to be.

All right, so good things aren't really happening with this first option.

Here's something else Sabrina could try: she could increase her one-on-one meetings with Bob and give him a safe environment to get his questions answered and address his concerns.

Let's look at the consequences of this option:

Short-Term Consequences
- Bob meets with Sabrina and vents about his concerns.

Long-Term Consequences
- Bob feels like he was treated fairly and given the freedom to work through his resistance, so he gets on board and becomes a champion, and he even helps find additional ways to build "stuff" better and faster for a lower cost.
- Alternatively, Bob finds another job because his resistance to Company A is deeply rooted in issues that cannot be addressed. However, he leaves Stuff & Co., Inc. on good terms because he was treated fairly.

In this option, Sabrina might lose Bob, but even if she does, she preserves the partnership with Company A and a sense of goodwill and good feelings at Stuff & Co., Inc. Again, Sabrina has found her way to a win-win option: by treating Bob fairly, she is able to preserve the partnership and avoid immense employee dissatisfaction.

Chapter 2: *Thoughtful*

Now that we've run through a multitude of examples, you should have a very good idea of what being thoughtful means, not only in theory but also in practice.

But I want to break it down even further for you now.

LETS GO! Be Thoughtful Leaders
1. Make a choice to think things through.
    a. Following positive examples and considering various consequences means that you're thinking things through.
    b. Not thinking things through means that you're making decisions on the fly.
    c. Taking enough time. I don't think there's necessarily a right or a wrong amount of time. It's all about really thinking things through, considering all of the possible angles, and then making a confident decision. Give yourself enough time to consider the following questions in order to cover all your bases:
        - How will this impact the employee?
        - How will this impact the team?
        - How will this impact the business?

- How will this impact me? (An emotionally mature and thoughtful leader will think of him- or herself last. But make sure you do think about yourself! After all, you're a member of the team, too, and negatively impacting you will also negatively impact others. You are important!)
2. Focus on Win-Win Options
   a. This one might sound tough, and it can be, because often the thoughtful responses balance a few negative/undesirable (and often short-term) consequences in order to ultimately gain bigger and better positive/desirable (often long-term) consequences.
   b. Sometimes it might also be difficult to figure out what the win-win option is, but Sabrina has worked it out over at Stuff & Co., Inc., so hopefully you have gotten a sense of how it's done. Ask yourself, how do I make all people involved happy? Go through options individually; figure out what will make each person happy. Then, see if you can piece all of those strategies together into one, and you'll be well on your way to a win-win result.

Chapter 2: Thoughtful

3. Choose to Empower and Engage
    a. A basketball coach engages with his players by asking them questions and listening to what they have to say. Sabrina does the same and empowers her employees by giving them the tools necessary to succeed. Having a safe environment is of the utmost importance so that employees feel welcome and secure in having their questions answered and concerns addressed.
    b. Empowering, engaging, and providing safe environments are key to thoughtful behavior.

Now you have everything you need in order to be an emotionally mature and thoughtful leader, putting you one step closer to full mastery of the LETS GO! framework. Stay with me, and you'll have the rest of it down in no time.

Chapter 3: Smart

"I never cut class. I loved getting A's; I liked being smart. I like being on time. I thought being smart is cooler than anything in the world."

– Michelle Obama,
First African-American First Lady of the United States

"You'd be surprised how many people think Non Compos Mentis is a degree."

Leaders are Emotionally Mature, Thoughtful, Smart, Goal-oriented, One-on-one practitioners

 Are you in the know about the company you keep, your customers, and your competitors?

You are now equipped with emotional maturity and thoughtfulness, so it's time to talk about the importance of being smart.

When I worked for a well-known accounting and consulting company, we had an opportunity to provide consulting services, valued at $40 million over three years, for a major air delivery and freight services company. We had very nearly crossed all our T's and dotted all our I's when a couple of unfortunate things happened. First, our Contracts Administration Team express mailed the revised contract using a competitor's service; think of it like sending FedEx something using a UPS envelope. Second, our Vice President of Sales, who felt he was God's gift to womankind, attempted to smooth things over by inappropriately flirting with one of the prospective company's female executives. Can you guess what happened? Yeah, we lost the contract.

This was a highly disappointing turn of events for everyone involved, myself included. If these leaders had just been smart about things, we would have gotten the contract. Like many

Chapter 3: Smart

people I know, I wish for the people who lead people to be smart.

The Oxford Dictionary notes the following synonyms for smart: clever, bright, intelligent, sharp-witted, quick-witted, shrewd, astute, able, perceptive, and percipient. Merriam-Webster defines being smart as being very good at learning or thinking about things; showing intelligence or good judgment. From these synonyms and definitions, we can see that showing the thoughtfulness that you developed in the last chapter gets you one step closer to achieving the kind of smarts necessary for leaders.

Which brings us to the next point: just what are business smarts? Being smart in general is widely considered a positive trait, but when I talk about needing to be smart as a leader, I don't mean that you just need to be good at a lot of math or science!

On December 16, 2013, Forbes published Rich Karlgaard's article titled "Smarts In Business Is Not About IQ." My favorite quote in the article comes from NetApp's CEO Tom Georgens who, while discussing smarts, said, "I know this irritates a lot of people, but once someone is at a certain point in his or her career—and it's not that far out, maybe five years—all the grades and academic credentials in the world don't mean anything anymore. It's all about accomplishment from that point on." NetApp is a $6.3 billion data storage company.

Being smart is about what you know in order to get things done, which just so happens to tie nicely into the next component of the LETS GO! framework: being goal-oriented. We explore goals in the next chapter.

Being smart comes down to a level of knowledge necessary to get things done. In Chapter 1, we talked about how important it is to know yourself and know your employees. That knowledge allows you to make informed, thoughtful decisions. It allows you to acknowledge any influences present in a given event. For business smarts, you also need to **know your company, your customers, and your competitors.**

We'll return to Sabrina over at Stuff & Co., Inc. in order to explore the various things you as a leader need to know about your company.

Company Vision and Values

What is the vision that drives your company? What are the values that fuel that vision? Often, these elements work in tandem, and you can't be aware of only one. As is a constant theme in this book, you need all the pieces of the puzzle;

Chapter 3: Smart

incomplete knowledge results in incomplete and insufficient responses.

Here, we'll use the Merriam-Webster definition of vision as "a thought, concept, or object formed by the imagination." Upon first glance, vision might sound too whimsical, but I think it fits just right. At some point during the inception of Stuff & Co., Inc., someone thought up the entire company, purely through his or her imagination. Then Stuff & Co., Inc. had a vision, a vision for what kind of company it wanted to be, what kind of future it wanted to have.

Sabrina needs to know the current vision (visions may change over time, so it's important to note if the company has changed direction) of Stuff & Co., Inc. At this point, you might be thinking that Sabrina should already know her company's mission! Well, I've got a sad truth to fill you in on: many companies spend a great deal of time creating strategy documents that include their vision, mission, values, and goals . . . but then the binders they put those ideas in (physical or virtual) sit on the shelf and remain virtually untouched.

Shouldn't everybody consult this information on a regular basis? Yes, absolutely. But few people do. Right now, Sabrina is one of the many people who haven't ever looked at those documents. But soon, she'll be a smart leader, one who knows the company she keeps.

Again, why does Sabrina need to make sure that she knows the current vision?

Well, Sabrina is in the midst of choosing between two different actions for Stuff & Co., Inc. Stuff & Co., Inc. has some extra money, and Sabrina has to decide whether to reinvest it in the company for further profit or give it to charity.

Without proper knowledge of the company's vision, how can she possibly make an informed decision?

Sabrina, being a very profit-driven manager, is tempted to reinvest in the business. However, first she sits down and ensures that she's being emotionally mature and thoughtful about the choice. She feels that she is. She's balanced the short-term and long-term consequences of both options and feels certain in her desire to reinvest in the business.

But then Sabrina remembers that she also has to be smart. She realizes that she needs to dust off the company's strategy document and revisit the company's vision. It was mentioned during orientation, but it is rarely discussed or reviewed. That's a problem!

With a bit of digging around, Sabrina finds out that one element of Stuff & Co., Inc.'s current

Chapter 3: Smart

vision is providing for its community in tangible ways.

Sabrina realizes that she could spin either reinvesting in the business or donating to charity as beneficial to the community. Reinvesting in the business would improve the business so that it could more readily provide for the community. Donating to charity would be an obvious way to contribute to the community.

She's torn. Then she remembers that her company's vision is based on a set of values, but she doesn't know what those values are. With a little digging around, Sabrina finds Stuff & Co., Inc.'s values: helping those in need, acting for the benefit of others, and never prioritizing business over individual needs. How lucky Sabrina is to work for such a gracious company!

Sabrina has a more comprehensive knowledge of Stuff & Co., Inc. now, enabling her to make the most informed decision possible. Weighing both the company's vision and values, it becomes obvious to her that she should donate the money to charity. This exercises and demonstrates Sabrina's emotional maturity, because it goes against her preference to reinvest in the company. She is donating the money to charity not because it suits her personal inclinations or desires but because she respects the company and knows that she is acting on its behalf, not for herself.

See what would have happened if Sabrina hadn't bothered to find out both the company's vision and values? She would have moved forward with a decision that would have gone against Stuff & Co., Inc.'s core values, making the company seem uncommitted to its vision.

Company Mission and Goals

Oftentimes, companies have a mission statement, and that mission statement is to be achieved by setting multiple goals of varying achievability levels.

Goals can be broken down a couple different ways. You can think of them in terms of immediate goals versus long-term goals or easy-to-achieve goals versus difficult-to-achieve goals. From there, goals can be broken down into different departments of a business.

For example: a sales team might have a goal of selling a specific number of units whereas a customer service team might have a goal of getting excellent feedback from customer surveys. Both would be working towards the company's overall goals of becoming more profitable and reputable.

Chapter 3: Smart

Phew! That's a lot of stuff to consider. You should already be able to imagine how difficult it would be to be a good leader if you didn't know your company's goals!

Company Operations, Systems, and Processes

The theme here is: the more knowledge you have, the better.

Sabrina has found herself with another problem on her hands because she's not familiar enough with her company's operations.

Two employees have come to Sabrina over a dispute. A product has been manufactured, but there is a problem with the quality. The first employee insists that he followed procedure correctly but that the error still occurred, so the equipment must be faulty. The second employee disagrees and states that the first employee did Step 4 incorrectly.

How can Sabrina know who is right without first being aware of the operations in place and the process that dictates how employees should work in the assembly line?

For the sake of convenience, we'll ignore the issue of "he said, she said" and assume that both employees are being honest in their accounts; they merely disagree about what the process is and how it should be carried out.

What does Sabrina do now?

She needs to sit down and educate herself so that she knows everything about the process in dispute. Once she has that key knowledge, she can easily determine how to facilitate an optimal solution.

Sabrina is sure learning a lot today, and she's becoming a better leader for it!

Company Products and Services

This covers the final section of the knowledge base of your company that every leader should have.

When it comes to products and services, you should be asking yourself the following question: how do or can our products and services add value to our current and future customers' lives? How can they do that seven minutes from now? Seven days from now? Seven weeks from now? Seven months from now? Seven years from now? Pick a number, any number, and keep asking yourself these questions. Having the answers on hand and in mind is key to being aware of what your company provides.

You should make sure that you have solid knowledge of your company's products and services and, even further, how those products and services address a need or want or solve a

Chapter 3: Smart

problem both today and in the future. Be an educated and authentic advocate of the services and/or products your company provides.

Let's check in with Sabrina. She is attending a charity fundraiser on behalf of Stuff & Co., Inc. During a casual dinner conversation, a prospective customer discusses a challenge his company is facing.

Is Sabrina aware of Stuff & Co., Inc.'s new service offering that would be an ideal solution for her dinner companion?

If Sabrina hasn't invested time in familiarizing herself with Stuff & Co., Inc.'s various offerings, then she won't be able to help this man or get new business.

However, if she has familiarized herself with the services, then she'll be able to authentically advocate on behalf of her company. This man will have a solution in front of him, and Sabrina will have drummed up some new business. Cheers all around! Again, the key here is that Sabrina keeps herself informed. If she doesn't, then all she'll get are lost opportunities.

Customers

I'm sure we're all familiar with the adage "the customer is always right." I don't want to entirely dismiss that, but I want you to think of it another way. Instead, consider "customers are the real bosses." If you use that adage instead, situations you may find yourself in won't rely on any notion of rightness but rather on how you can best serve any customer right in front of you, since that is who you answer to.

As a leader, you have the responsibility of setting this example. Sabrina, too, has this responsibility.

Of course, running with the theme, how can Sabrina serve her customers well if she doesn't know them? Any given customer base will be different on the macro level (according to demographics such as age and wealth) and then on the micro level (according to the customers' varying personalities).

In this day and age, it's actually pretty easy to keep an eye on what customers are thinking about their experiences and interactions with businesses. For example, Yelp has provided a forum for people to express their opinions and state whether or not they would recommend a business to a friend. The system takes word of mouth to a whole other level.

In general, all social media serves this function. Consumers and customers use social media sites such as Twitter, Facebook, and Yelp to share their opinions—which could be positive or negative. By having a social media presence, your company will be able to keep an eye on these sites and take a look at customers' actual feedback.

In addition, your business could incorporate voluntary, creatively distributed customer surveys that request feedback. This would also help you see if you were meeting your customers' needs.

Competitors

Keep an eye on your competition and ask yourself the following questions: What need or want are they satisfying? Is it the same need or want that we should be satisfying? How are they doing it? Why are they doing it? Are their solutions more creative or innovative than ours? Are they making any part of the customer's journey easier? How do our customers feel about our competitors? Would our employees prefer to work for them over us?

It's a lot to keep track of, but ultimately you can learn a lot about your own company by watching your competitors'. You can also even pick up some tricks!

Don't forget to be thoughtful, though, because competition may come from many varied and possibly unexpected sources. Some investigation may be in order to discover some of your competitors.

Sabrina thinks that Stuff & Co., Inc. has no competition because it has been the industry leader for more than 20 years. Is it smart for Sabrina to think this way?

Certainly not! It's really quite foolish for Sabrina to think this way. Because she has made an assumption and not objectively researched their competitors, Sabrina has missed the fact that her company does indeed have a number of competitors that she could or should learn a lot about.

To sum this all up in a quick way: know your company, your customers, and your competitors.

It's certainly a lot of information to know, and on top of it all, you should keep yourself apprised of current events in the business world and keep an eye out for interesting research that may change the landscape. Thankfully, there are many resources to help leaders get a better handle on all of this information!

I know you're stretched for time as it is, so I've compiled the following table as a helpful guide that you can consult in order to keep working on your knowledge base.

Chapter 3: Smart

Resource	Website	Twitter Handle	Description
Business Week	www.businessweek.com	@BW	Business news
Fast Company	www.fastcompany.com	@FastCompany	Innovation in the business place
Forbes	www.forbes.com	@Forbes	Information center for business leaders
Forrester Research	www.forrester.com	@Forrester	Research and analysis of companies, products, services, and many industries
Fortune Magazine	www.fortune.com	@FortuneMagazine	Business news
Harvard Business Review	www.hbr.org	@HarvardBiz	Business articles, case studies, etc.
Hoover's (a D&B company)	www.hoovers.com	@Hoovers	Database of company and business information
Inc Magazine	www.inc.com	@inc	Articles oriented towards small businesses
Mashable	www.mashable.com	@mashable	News website
McKinsey Research	www.mckinsey.com/insights/	@McKinsey_MGI	Articles related to leadership
New York Times	www.nytimes.com	@nytimes	News
Soundview	www.summary.com	@BusinessBooks	Executive book summaries
TechCrunch	www.techcrunch.com	@TechCrunch	Technology news
The Nielsen Wire	www.nielsen.com	@Nielsen	Tracks what people watch, listen to, and buy
The Wall Street Journal	www.online.wsj.com	@WSJ	Business news

Leaders are Emotionally Mature, Thoughtful, Smart, Goal-oriented, One-on-one practitioners

I suggest that you familiarize yourself with all of these resources and then add to the list or subtract from it as needed. They are quality business publications that are well respected within the community. Again, remember that the more you know, the better!

LETS GO! be smart leaders who are in the know, who know the company they keep (yourself, your boss, employees, peers, and company), know that their customers are the real bosses, and know their competitors. Those things equip us with the knowledge we need to really succeed!

Chapter 4: Goal-Oriented

"People with goals succeed because they know where they're going."

– Earl Nightingale, *American motivational speaker and author*

"And then, in seven years and three months and fourteen days and two and one-half hours, our extremely careful planning will pay off."

***L**eaders are **E**motionally Mature, **T**houghtful, **S**mart,
Goal-oriented, **O**ne-on-one practitioners*

"I always wanted to be something, but now I see I should have been more specific."

– Lily Tomlin, *American actress, comedian, producer, and writer*

 Do you know where you are going?

Let's really think through this question and consider Tomlin's quote above. If you think you know where you're going, ask yourself: do I really? Am I being specific enough? These are important questions to pose to yourself on a regular basis because it's pretty hard to get anywhere you want to be if you're uncertain of your destination.

A useful way of thinking about knowing where you're going and how to set goals is to consider taking a trip. First, where do you want to go on your trip? If you don't have a clear destination in mind, then you could end up anywhere; you could easily end up somewhere you didn't want to be! So first, pick your destination. Then ask yourself: what is the best route for me to reach this destination? Again, in terms of a trip, this would involve consulting maps and deciding on modes of travel and other such things. In doing

Chapter 4: Goal-Oriented

this, you have broken down your goal into small, achievable steps. Such a breakdown is an imperative part of the process to be a goal-oriented leader.

To stress the point further: it is impossible to achieve positive results if you do not have a crystal clear picture of the goal. However, goals can be and often are difficult, so in this chapter, I want to make the daunting process much easier for you. Here, I'm going to introduce you to a new kind of SMART: **S**pecific, **M**easurable, **A**ttainable, **R**elevant, and **T**ime-bound goals. We talked about being smart in the previous chapter. Now we're considering SMART in a different way —as it combines directly with the goal-oriented part of the LETS GO! formula. Remember, everything fits together, and you need foundational smarts before you can get these SMARTs.

Many attribute the term SMART to Peter Drucker (1954) or George T. Doran (November 1981, *Management Review*). The primary advantage of SMART goals is that they are easier to understand, do, and then be reassured that they have been done. And we like easy! Easier goals will translate into a higher number of achieved goals. As with most helpful things, the process of outlining and accomplishing SMART

*L*eaders are *E*motionally Mature, *T*houghtful, *S*mart,
*G*oal-oriented, *O*ne-on-one practitioners

goals is simple; the challenge lies in being deliberate and intentional about doing them. SMART goals won't just achieve themselves, after all!

My favorite reminder is getting and staying fit. Managing your health and exercise lifestyle is easily one of the most daunting things you can do. So I approach it with SMART goals. Most of the time, I use the 80/20 rule for eating healthy and balanced meals, sleeping well, exercising, and minimizing negative stress.

> The 80/20 rules comes from quality management pioneer Dr. Joseph Juran. In the 1930s and 1940s, he recognized a universal principle that he called the "vital few and trivial many"—essentially that 20% of something is responsible for 80% of the results.
>
> The 80/20 rule (or as I like to say, the 80/20/80 rule) then can serve as a constant companion to remind you to spend 80% of your time on the most important 20% of your work because it will produce 80% of your desired results.

For example, countless wellness and fitness experts emphasize the overwhelming importance of eating meals that are healthy and balanced (the most important 20% of the process). So, I try to focus 80% of my effort and energy on eating right because it will produce 80% of my desired wellness and fitness goals. If you think that one of the other components (sleep, exercise, stress, etc.) is the most important part, you should spend 80% of your energy on that component instead.

Chapter 4: Goal-Oriented

When I put it that way, it sounds simple, so why don't we all do it? Motivation and ability are certainly factors at play, and we will discuss those in the next chapter. For now, we'll focus on breaking the components down.

The SMART mnemonic acronym has evolved over time and continues to be incredibly useful to leaders. It's worth noting that some people use variants of this acronym in which some letters will stand for different words; other people will even add in some extra letters. I like to stick to the original formula, but all versions have something helpful to offer.

Let's break down each of the components of the SMART system. First, I will give you a basic, working definition of each component. Then, I will give you a series of questions that are associated with putting each component into practice. Finally, I will show you each component in action through an example.

Specific

A specific goal is one that is clearly defined or identified. By asking yourself the following questions, you should be able to incorporate specificity.

*Leaders are Emotionally Mature, Thoughtful, Smart,
Goal-oriented, One-on-one practitioners*

- What do I want to accomplish?
- Why do I want to accomplish it?
- Who will be/is involved?
- Where will this take place?
- Which requirements and constraints will affect this goal?

Let's return first to my example of staying healthy. That's not very specific, is it? Staying healthy could mean a lot of different things. Instead of being vague, I need to outline the who, what, why, when, and where. My revised goal is: lower my bad cholesterol by eating a full three servings of vegetables every day and working out at the gym four days a week.

    The **who** is me. The **why** is for the sake of my health. The **what** is lowering my bad cholesterol. The **when** is during every meal. The **where** is anywhere I eat meals and at the gym.

    I haven't yet considered any requirements and/or constraints that would affect this goal. You may not have any to consider, which is helpful. But, for example, if I had a sprained ankle, that would directly impact my ability to perform certain kinds of exercises, and I would need to consider it when planning how to achieve this goal.

Chapter 4: Goal-Oriented

You should be able to see the difference between the initial goal (get healthy) and the revised, more specific goal (reduce bad cholesterol levels by specific actions).

Let's see how Sabrina over at Stuff & Co., Inc. can make her goal more specific. Stuff & Co., Inc. has its fingers in lots of different business. One of its branches is a chain of retail stores. However, right now the retail stores aren't performing particularly well. Sabrina's initial goal is to increase Stuff & Co., Inc.'s retail business. But increasing business could mean a lot of things! So, she has to go through those questions and figure out how to make her goal more specific.

What? More business. What does Sabrina mean by more business?
- She has to think hard on this one, as you often will. It's very easy to conceive of vague goals, and much harder to conceive of specific goals.
- Once she thinks it through, Sabrina realizes that her goal is to increase sales by 10%.

Why? Sabrina wants to increase sales by 10% so that the company will be more profitable.

Who? Sabrina finds this question a bit tougher. She'll likely need to involve many people for this goal. It can be useful to break it down in terms of team goals vs. individual goals. Certainly, Sabrina shouldn't rely on one individual to boost sales by 10%, so instead, she will make it the priority of one specific team—the sales team! And she is involved too.

Where? Meetings can be held at Stuff & Co., Inc.'s corporate offices.

Which? Sabrina thinks long and hard about any potential constraints and decides that there aren't any, so long as she doesn't place them herself. As the goal-maker, Sabrina has control over the various elements of the goal, including timeframe, which will be covered later. It is useful for Sabrina to keep thinking about potential constraints so that she does not create any that she doesn't want in place.

Now Sabrina is ready with her brand new and revised goal: to have the sales team increase Stuff & Co., Inc.'s sales by 10%. Much, much better than simply "increase business."

All right, so now you've got a specific goal. But remember, that's not the only component of the SMART goal system. There are more to go.

Measurable

A measurable goal is one that is capable of being measured. Sounds obvious, right? It's the kind of definition that spins back on itself. Some synonyms

Chapter 4: Goal-Oriented

might be helpful for further understanding. A measurable goal is noticeable, visible, perceptible. Essentially, it needs to produce results that can be seen in some quantifiable way. To do that, ask yourself the following questions:

- How much?
- How many?
- How will I know when it is accomplished?
- In what quantifiable ways can I measure success?

Now that Sabrina's goal is specifically to increase sales by 10%, she realizes that she has already made her goal measurable. This is good! Often, making the goal specific solves a lot of the other steps. If not, don't worry.

For example, if I have a personal goal of being more productive, I might clarify that and make it specific by changing it to a goal of completing more work tasks every day. That, however, still isn't quantifiable. So I ask myself, just how many more tasks do I want to achieve every day? My answer would then be: I want to complete two more tasks each day than I am currently doing now. Once I've decided that, I can measure whether or not I actually complete two more tasks each day than my previous average.

***L**eaders are **E**motionally **M**ature, **T**houghtful, **S**mart,
Goal-oriented, **O**ne-on-one practitioners*

Attainable

An attainable goal must be achievable. For different people, this will mean different things. For example, few goals will have a 100% chance of being achievable, especially if they take place within certain time frames. For example, one goal might only have roughly a 75% chance of being completed in six months but a 95% chance of being completed in ten months.

It's ultimately up to you to know what's achievable and what isn't. In order to do so, you need to have the necessary knowledge (i.e. the capabilities of you and your team). Ask yourself this one question:

- How can the goal be accomplished?

At this stage with her goal-making, Sabrina realizes that perhaps a 10% increase in sales is too much pressure. By reflecting on how to achieve the goal and all of the strategies involved, she revises the goal to a 7.5% increase in sales. Now she feels it is more attainable. If she wants, she can always make an additional goal in the future to continue increasing sales.

Relevant

A relevant goal must be closely connected or appropriate to the matter at hand. Ask yourself:
- Does this seem worthwhile?
- Is this the right time?
- Does this goal match my individual/company efforts/needs?
- Am I the right person to carry out this goal?
- Is this goal applicable in the current socio-economic and technical environment?

Relevance is very important to the goal-maker. Sabrina must ask herself: is this the right thing to be focusing on right now? Should she instead focus, perhaps, on providing better customer service? Again, this requires Sabrina to have the necessary smarts or knowledge about her business, Stuff & Co., Inc.

Sabrina goes through these questions and decides that yes, it is the right time, it matches the company's needs, and she is the right person to carry out the goal. If she could not answer yes to all those questions, then she would need to start over from the beginning with a different goal, one that was more relevant.

Leaders are Emotionally Mature, Thoughtful, Smart, Goal-oriented, One-on-one practitioners

Time-Bound

A time-bound goal is one that has a time constraint of some sort placed on it. It doesn't do you too much good to write a goal that is specific, measurable, attainable, and relevant if you say to yourself that you'll just get it done whenever. Instead, know when you want to have your goal completed and break it down into steps along the way. The following questions will help you think of your goal in relation to time:

- When will these steps be carried out?
- What can I do six months from now?
- What can I do six weeks from now?
- What can I do today?

This is the tricky part. Sabrina knows she wants to increase sales by 7.5%, and she feels that it is a relevant and attainable goal. However, she could easily make the goal unattainable if she sought to complete it in two days. She must consider under what timeframe she wants to complete the goal.

Sabrina runs through these questions and gets a bit stuck on the first one. When will these steps be carried out? She realizes she doesn't have any steps! And that's a problem. Right now, she just has one big goal of increasing sales, and that needs to be broken down into steps. So she sits

Chapter 4: Goal-Oriented

and thinks about it. She even gets some help from the sales team, because incorporating the thoughts and expertise of her coworkers is an essential part of the process to create SMART goals. (Remember: an emotionally mature and thoughtful leader considers other opinions.)

Collectively, Sabrina and the sales team decide that Step 1 will be to plan some store events. Step 2 will be to create a rewards program that provides incentives for loyal customers to keep returning to Stuff & Co., Inc. Step 3 will be to create an advertising campaign to make consumers aware of the store events. Finally, Step 4 will be to enroll 50% of customers who attend the store events and encourage them to use word of mouth to recruit new customers.

Now that Sabrina has a set of steps, she can decide when each step will be carried out. She can figure out what she can do today (start planning), what she can do in six weeks (begin working on the advertising campaign), and what she can do in six months (hold the store events).

Sabrina has completed the SMART process in order to craft her goal and is much better off for it! Her team members appreciate that she used their input, and they feel confident in their ability to complete the goal (because it is attainable).

*Leaders are Emotionally Mature, Thoughtful, Smart,
Goal-oriented, One-on-one practitioners*

They also know just how to accomplish the goal (because it is specific, measured, and time-bound). Lastly, they know it is a worthwhile goal that will benefit Stuff & Co., Inc. upon completion (because it is relevant).

Phew! Sabrina would have been hard pressed to work all of that out without SMART goals.

Best of all, as Sabrina continues to practice making SMART goals, the process will become easier and easier. Before you know it, Sabrina will be the champion of SMART goals—which is good, because effective leaders are goal-oriented!

LETS GO! Be **G**oal-Oriented Leaders . . .
1. Involve others as you create and write SMART team and individual goals.
    a. Working completely on your own leaves you blind to valuable input that your colleagues can offer you.
2. Review your SMART goals daily or weekly.
    a. The more you consult SMART goals, the better. Looking over them will remind you of your current task as well as your ultimate objective, keeping you motivated.

3. Adjust as needed.
    a. Unforeseen circumstances may throw a wrench in your plans, and that's okay. It just means that you'll need to revise your goal.
    b. It's important to keep your goal updated as needed so that it remains relevant and attainable!

Chapter 5: One-on-One Practitioner

"The things that make me different are the things that make me."

– A.A. Milne, *English Author*

"I'm tired of not talking about me. Can we just get back to talking about me?"

Leaders are Emotionally Mature, Thoughtful, Smart, Goal-oriented, One-on-one practitioners

 Is it fair to treat everyone the same?

A **L**eader who is **E**motionally mature, **T**houghtful, **S**mart, and **G**oal-oriented has a lot going for him or her. Now, he or she can tackle the last piece of the LETS GO! framework by becoming a one-on-one practitioner.

A leader should always value the people whom he or she leads. That is the basis behind becoming a one-on-one practitioner. A practitioner is one who practices continually; holding one-on-one sessions and being an effective communicator are things that you will have to continue to practice as you travel along your leadership journey; you can't just try them once and be done.

> "We see them come. We see them go. Some are fast. And some are slow. **Not one of them is like another.**"
> One Fish, Two Fish, Red Fish, Blue Fish by Dr. Seuss

Once you have the right attitude, you can deploy one of the most important (if not the most important) leadership tools: the ability to facilitate well-prepared, goal-oriented, and focused one-on-one meetings.

This sounds scary to a lot of people. It's likely that many of you wonderful readers have never

Chapter 5: One-on-One Practitioner

had a one-on-one meeting with an employee. However, such meetings create opportunities that are invaluable to your leadership, and so I implore you to at least continue reading with this chapter. Afterwards, try it out to see for yourself. I guarantee that one-on-one meetings will make a huge difference in your work environment.

Why do I make such bold claims? Well, every employee is different, and the best way to develop each is to give each individual attention. Group meetings, while useful and great for certain purposes, do not address individual needs. I think (and am convinced that most others would agree) that effective communication, both oral and written, is the lifeblood of a successful organization and of relationships in general. So ask yourself: how many hours a day do I spend communicating?

Imagine if no one communicated. It's nearly impossible to visualize because we always communicate, at least non-verbally. We can't help ourselves. Human interaction boils down to communication. I'm sure you've heard the old adage "It's not what you say but how you say it." Can you imagine if every time you communicated something to someone, your recipient fully understood your intended message, whether simple or complex or somewhere in between?

*Leaders are **E**motionally Mature, **T**houghtful, **S**mart,
Goal-oriented, **O**ne-on-one practitioners*

That's what one-on-one sessions seek to accomplish.

To effectively coach and communicate with employees to develop them so that they are productive, happy workers, you must talk to them face-to-face, one-on-one. And don't forget: as a leader, this is the essence of your job—to take care of a group of people. With crystal clear expectations, SMART goals, and guiding values and principles, your employees will continue to grow and improve in order to help accomplish your organization's goals.

When it comes to scheduling, things can be a bit complicated. There's no one-size-fits-all approach. In fact, that would go precisely against the individual attention one-on-ones are designed to provide! Based on each employee's preferences and responsibilities, you may meet at different frequencies and for different lengths. With one employee, you may meet every week for five minutes. With another employee, you may meet twice a month for twenty minutes. If you lead people in different locations, you may opt for video chats or phone calls. If you work electronically, you may set aside the time for quick online text chats or set up weekly email correspondence.

Chapter 5: One-on-One Practitioner

Again, I know this sounds daunting. One manufacturing supervisor who had 30 direct reports once told me it would be impossible for him to meet face-to-face with his assembly worker team. I suggested the following and told him that if the one-on-ones did not improve his relationships with his team within three months, I would get him courtside tickets to an NBA game. (Have I ever mentioned how useful incentives are?) Also notice that I didn't say I was going to *buy* him the tickets; I've got some connections that have been very useful for this sort of thing.

If you're facing the challenge of struggling to create useful incentives and reward programs, just ask your employees! I wouldn't have known that basketball tickets were an appropriate incentive for this supervisor if I had never bothered to notice (or be alert to the fact) that he was a big basketball fan.

I told him to start by giving his team the following message during a group stand-up meeting:

"I want to be a better leader, and part of that includes staying connected to each one of you so that I can set you up for success and remove obstacles as needed. For three months, I plan to pick one of you each day and meet with you for one minute when you arrive or before a break or any other mutually agreed upon time and location. I will use a stopwatch. For 20 to 30 seconds, I will share what I think you are doing well to contribute to the team and organizational goals. Then, I will ask what I can do to help you focus on what you do best. And finally, I will ask how I can help you overcome challenges or remove obstacles. For the other 30 to 40 seconds, you can talk about anything you'd like."

Of course, I told him to say it in his own words. He essentially informed his employees of his attempts to become a one-on-one expert and detailed how he would accomplish that.

Did it work?

You bet it did! And it has worked for countless other people who lead people. Otherwise, I wouldn't be working so hard to convince you that being a one-on-one practitioner is so valuable. In three months, this manager met with each one of his employees at least three times, sometimes more. He now keeps regularly scheduled one-on-ones with his team. Some for one minute each week, some longer, and some more frequently, based on what his employees need.

Notice here that you have a positive feedback loop. Once you've met with an employee for the first time, you will better understand his or her needs. Over time, you can work to meet those needs; and as you continue to meet, you will improve the working relationship. Productivity and overall employee satisfaction went way up for this manager, and the rumor mill died down. It's a beautiful thing when leaders chat with their people. And I even got him two NBA courtside tickets, despite winning the bet!

Personality Profiling

Once you're willing to set up these one-on-one meetings, you'll find that there's some knowledge that you need. You need to understand the preferences and profiles of each one of your employees. This harkens all the way back to being emotionally mature!

There are three different approaches often used to create a profile for a person. I often ask people what personality or profile assessment they use for their businesses. Over the last four years, I have seen more than 2,000 people who attended a business skills workshop I taught, giving me a large pool to draw from. I am going to list for you the most frequent responses.

The first is the DiSC profile (Dominance, Influence, Steadiness, Conscientiousness). The second is the MBTI (Myers-Briggs Type Indicator).

The third is Gallup's Strengths Finder. All three assessments will illuminate a lot of a person's traits. I enjoy being aware of all three, but it is perfectly reasonable to use just one, which is what most people do.

I want to give you a quick overview of each of these personality assessment methods, so that you can consider which might be best for you. I strongly recommend that you participate in at least one of them. It's difficult to know yourself, and these tests take some of the mystery out of it!

First, we'll cover the DiSC profiles. The official website, which contains a lot of information as well as all products, is www.everythingdisc.com. Tests can be purchased for individuals ($89) or for larger company-wide teams. Taking the DiSC assessment requires answering a number of questions; your answers to those questions are what make up your results. Depending on your results, you may get one or more of the following types: Dominance, Influence, Steadiness, Conscientiousness. DiSC has a global network of partners from whom you can purchase assessments and services to help you or your organization along the DiSC journey. My colleagues and I are DiSC partners, as we have found it very helpful over the years, but the goal

Chapter 5: One-on-One Practitioner

of this book is to give an unbiased overview of how a number of different assessment tools work and could help you.

Here are the types:

Dominance. A person who receives the dominance type is one who sees the big picture, is not afraid of being blunt, accepts challenges, gets straight to the point, and places emphasis on accomplishing results/the bottom line.

Influence. A person who receives the influence type is one who shows enthusiasm, is optimistic, enjoys collaborating, dislikes being ignored, and places emphasis on openness and relationships.

Steadiness. A person who receives the steadiness type does not like to be rushed, takes supportive actions, practices humility, and places emphasis on sincerity, cooperation, and dependability.

Conscientiousness. A person who receives the conscientious type enjoys independence, employs objective reasoning, wants the details, fears being wrong, and places emphasis on quality, accuracy, and competency.

Remember, a person may receive any number of these types. For example, Sabrina is a Di. She has both the dominance and the influence types, which results in her being extremely driven and focused on achieving success through collaborative efforts.

You get more detailed feedback if you participate in a DiSC profile assessment. For example, if Stuff & Co., Inc. invested in an Everything DiSC Management Profile for Sabrina, then her personalized report would include the following: Sabrina's DiSC style, priorities, management preferences, motivators, and stressors. It would also include information about how to direct and delegate with the different D, I, S, and C styles, the environment she creates with her styles, her approach to developing the styles, how she is perceived by her manager, and how to work with managers of the various styles.

Let's move on to the MBTI assessments. The test (www.myersbriggs.org) can be taken online but costs around $150 (it comes with personal feedback). There are also a number of MBTI Master Practitioners who can be hired and brought in to the business place.

Upon taking the assessment, you will be presented with results that give you one of the 16 different personality types. The Myers-Briggs personality assessment builds off of C.G. Jung's psychological types and seeks to interpret them in ways that will be useful to us. Your personality type is built from the four different Jungian profiles. Each of the four parts has two different possibilities:

Extraversion (E) or Introversion (I). This first section will tell you whether you prefer to focus on the outer world of people and things or the inner world of ideas and images. Often, people already identify themselves as either extroverts or introverts, so this category can be very easy to interpret.

Sabrina, for example, knows that she is an extrovert. She has always enjoyed engaging with the outer world and making connections with other people. Upon taking the MBTI, this is confirmed and her personality type starts with the letter "E."

Sensing (S) or Intuition (N). This category has to do with information processing. One who is sensing focuses on basic information and facts presented, whereas one who is intuitive takes information as an opportunity to interpret and add meaning.

Sabrina wasn't sure which of these she would score as, prior to taking the MBTI. When she did, she received sensing, and so now her personality type reads "ES." She understands the results because she can see how the way she answered certain questions indicated this about her. It's a pretty cool experience!

Thinking (T) or Feeling (F). This category has to do with the decision-making process we all undergo. One who is thinking approaches decisions with logic and consistency, whereas one who is feeling approaches decisions from the standpoint of the people involved and whatever special circumstances might apply.

Sabrina felt pretty confident that she would receive thinking, because she knows she has a logical mind, and she does. So now her personality type reads "EST."

Judging (J) or Perceiving (P). This category has to do with how you react to the outside world. One who is judging prefers to get things decided quickly. One who is perceiving prefers to stay open to new information and options.

For the final category, Sabrina receives judging, which completes her personality types as ESTJ. Now that she has the full four letters, she can learn a bit more about what it all means. Just skimming the surface, she learns that she is an active organizer, logical, assertive, concrete, critical, and responsible.

To compare and contrast a little bit, Sabrina has a colleague named Salem, who is an INTP. He's almost entirely the opposite type! Keywords

Chapter 5: One-on-One Practitioner

for him indicate that he's logical, conceptual, detached, and critical. Furthermore, he loves ideas and pursues understanding. So, you can see where there is some overlap between Sabrina and Salem. They are both logical and critical. However, they differ quite a lot from there. But now that Sabrina and Salem both know their types, they will be better prepared for how to interact with each other.

Last but not least, I want to make quick mention of Gallup's Strengths Finder. According to Gallup, people who use their strengths every day are six times more likely to be engaged on the job. This assessment tool helps people identify their unique combination of skills, talents, and knowledge—also known as strengths. For $9.99, you can discover your top five strengths and for $89.99 you can discover all 34 of your strengths. More information can be found on their website at www.gallupstrengthscenter.com.

On top of having various personality types, your employees will also, generally speaking, fall into one of the four categories in the table below. Knowing where each employee falls in this table is also essential for the one-on-one meetings. This table deals with the intersection of employee motivation and capability.

*Leaders are **E**motionally Mature, **T**houghtful, **S**mart, **G**oal-oriented, **O**ne-on-one practitioners*

	I do not want to contribute to the team and company	I want to contribute to the team and company
I can do it	Indicates a motivation or resistance challenge. There are solutions!	Superstar employee!
I cannot do it	No solution.	Indicates a learning or development challenge. There are solutions!

If you have an employee who does not want to do a certain job AND cannot do a certain job, then it is your duty to respectfully help him or her find another job. There are no solutions there; it's the bad square. While I believe that everyone has a purpose and adds value in some capacity, some people are just in the wrong job. For whatever reason, they don't want the job they have, and they can't complete the job they have. I understand that some people work solely to pay the bills, but even then, employees should be held accountable to guiding values and

Chapter 5: One-on-One Practitioner

principles. At minimum, that means doing your job and being a respectful team player.

On the opposite end of the spectrum, if you have an employee who both can and wants to do the job, then you're in the clear! That's exactly the kind of employee that you want, which is why that box gets a star.

However, we don't want to overlook the employees in the other two boxes. If an employee can do a job but does not want to, then you should address that in one-on-one meetings with that employee and inquire about ways you can increase his or her motivation. If you have another employee who wants to do a job but cannot, you should also address that in one-on-one meetings. You could ask that employee what help he or she needs in order to improve his or her skills and gain mastery over the job.

No matter what kind of people you're dealing with, whatever their personality profiles or capabilities, the key to being a one-on-on expert is communication. Create a baseline of communication. Communicate again, and then communicate some more. Just like with patience, you can't have too much communication.

Effective communication is timely, targeted, and tailored. It should have a rhythm and cadence that moves the recipient. Conventional wisdom says that we should communicate a message 5 to 7 times. My experience tells me it may feel like you have to say something 5 to 1,499 times, especially when you work with employees who have drastically different communication styles. Certain people will need to hear things more than others, and it is your responsibility to continue communicating until every employee gets it, within a reasonable amount of time.

Lastly, know what you prefer and what your employees prefer. Then compromise so that you do not drive each other crazy. Remember how Sabrina and Salem have such different MBTI types? Sometimes Sabrina has to compromise, and other times Salem does; either way, one of them needs to—otherwise they will just keep butting heads. Compromise is the emotionally mature thing to do.

Now I'd like to give you a sample of my effective meeting guidelines. This sample will help you in structuring your own meetings. The guidelines are based on my own extensive experience in working in one-on-one situations.

Chapter 5: One-on-One Practitioner

1:1 MEETING GUIDELINES (These are included on the agenda. They must be acknowledged and reviewed).
1. Foster a healthy, safe, open, and productive environment.
   a. Know yourself and your employees.
   b. Make sure the Vegas rule applies: what happens in the meeting stays in the meeting, and information does not get shared outside (unless there are serious Human Resource issues that need to be addressed). Your employees will not feel safe if they know that you gossip about them.
2. Be prepared (this applies both to you and to your employee).
   a. Participation is not optional.
   b. No one person is allowed to dominate the meeting; everyone is valuable and should be heard.
3. Practice active listening.
   a. This means you have to actively engage in what your employee is saying to you and make the effort to understand completely.

Leaders are Emotionally Mature, Thoughtful, Smart, Goal-oriented, One-on-one practitioners

4. Focus.
   a. Cell phones should not be allowed except in the case of emergency.
   b. You should adhere to the agenda as much as possible.
   c. If you aren't focused, then the one-on-one session will be derailed, and you won't accomplish what you want to.
5. Respect people's time.
   a. Time is money. Every minute past 5 minutes is an extra $5. Once you reach $25 (10 minutes), the meeting is automatically cancelled.
   b. Do not exceed the scheduled time, but do feel free to finish early if the purpose/objectives are met.
6. Allow time at the end to recap and document.
7. Follow up.
   a. It's important that your employees know you are accessible at other times. It is also important to check in with your employees outside of the meetings and make sure that the meeting went well.

With these guidelines in mind, let's look at a sample agenda:

AGENDA
1. Thanks.
   a. Share specific employee accomplishments.
      i. Try to pick accomplishments of all kinds—ones that are small, medium, and large. Make sure to note how they relate to short- and long-term goals.
   b. This step in the agenda is important in making the employee feel like a valued member of a team. It also lets the employee know what he or she is doing right.
2. Address questions, concerns, and rumor mill from group meetings or any other communications.
   a. You might find that, going into the meeting, you have certain pieces of gossip that you want to address.
   b. Other times, you might find that you aren't aware of any current questions or concerns, and so it is very, very important to ask the employee.

3. Ask the employee: what do you need from me in order for you to concentrate on what you do best? Focus on individual, team, and company goals.
    a. Again, the theme of the meeting is to ask the employee what he or she needs. The employee will know better than you.
4. Follow-up items.

These meeting guidelines and sample agenda are a great way of getting started, but you have to remember that every employee is different. Because every employee is different, you will have to use slightly different strategies in any given situation. Let's see how Sabrina is doing with her one-on-one interactions. She has two different employees who differ from her own type with whom she'll be meeting soon.

First, Sabrina, who is an I-type, will be meeting with her employee Suzanne, who is a C-type. What should her general approach be to creating a motivating environment for Suzanne? Recall that the Influence style (Sabrina) indicates one who shows enthusiasm, is optimistic, enjoys collaborating, dislikes being ignored, and places emphasis on openness and relationships. On the other hand, the Conscientiousness style

Chapter 5: One-on-One Practitioner

(Suzanne) enjoys independence, employs objective reasoning, wants to know details, fears being wrong, and places emphasis on quality, accuracy, and competency.

Sabrina, being an emotionally mature and thoughtful leader, is cognizant of their key differences: collaborative versus independent; optimistic versus cautious. Therefore, during her regularly scheduled one-on-one interactions with Suzanne, Sabrina makes an effort to share her expectations logically, clearly, and specifically, with minimal enthusiasm. Sabrina will focus on quality standards and give Suzanne ample time.

Sabrina is also going to be meeting with Salem soon. He is a D-type. What will Sabrina's general approach be to Salem's long-term professional development? Recall that the Dominance style indicates a person who sees the big picture, is not afraid of being blunt, accepts challenges, gets straight to the point, and places emphasis on accomplishing results/the bottom line.

Gallup research reminds us to focus on what we do best, so Sabrina will focus on development opportunities that showcase and develop Salem's strengths while also helping Stuff & Co., Inc. to accomplish its goals. Stuff & Co., Inc. has an initiative to quickly and with a sense of

*Leaders are Emotionally Mature, Thoughtful, Smart,
Goal-oriented, One-on-one practitioners*

urgency respond to a competitive threat that demands remarkable results. Sabrina thinks Salem is tailor-made to be the leader of this initiative precisely because of his D typology—because he is competitive, is comfortable being in charge, loves a challenge, and is driven by results. Sabrina will support Salem by helping him to think things through and stay focused.

Are you ready to be a one-on-one practitioner now? LETS GO!

1. Have regularly scheduled one-on-one meetings based on your employees' and your own preferences and needs.
2. Be prepared in your meetings.
3. Be focused in your meetings.
4. Follow up.

Chapter 6: LETS GO!

"With your head full of brains and your shoes full of feet, you're too smart to go down any not-so-good street."

– Dr. Seuss, *Oh the Places You'll Go!*

"I have a few complaints about how you're doing your job as my boss."

Leaders are Emotionally Mature, Thoughtful, Smart, Goal-oriented, One-on-one practitioners

Are you ready to lead with a LETS GO! state of mind?

Leaders are emotionally mature, thoughtful, smart, goal-oriented, and one-on-one practitioners. We've looked at how each of these components operate individually, and we've even seen how they build on one another to work together. Now, let's see how they all work together in action. Let's check in with Sabrina over at Stuff & Co., Inc.

Following the LETS GO! framework means constantly incorporating all of its components.

It's a Monday, and Sabrina is eager to apply the information she learned on Friday at the LETS GO! workshop. After she parks her car in the garage and heads toward the elevator, she greets every employee she meets. She knows them by name because she is thoughtful and has taken the time to familiarize herself with every member of her department. Sometimes it's a bit overwhelming, but everyone at Stuff & Co., Inc. appreciates the efforts that Sabrina goes through. She even knows that Jack likes his coffee black and Jennifer likes hers with cream!

Chapter 6: LETS GO!

Sabrina reaches the elevator and sees Owen standing there.

"Hi, Owen," she says and smiles brightly. She knows it's important that she shows enthusiasm for her work and approaches interactions with a positive attitude.

"Oh, hey, Sabrina." Owen fidgets nervously, hand gripping a to-go coffee from Starbucks.

"How are things going?" Sabrina asks. She last had a one-on-one meeting with Owen on Thursday, and they aren't due to meet again until this Thursday, but she knows the importance of following up with employees.

"Oh, you know. They're going," Owen responds.

"Have you been feeling good since our meeting? Is there anything that's come up since then?" Sabrina does her best to ask honest questions and keep herself receptive to whatever answer Owen might have. Of course, she hopes that Owen is still doing really well, but she's prepared to help him if he isn't.

"Yeah. I mean, some family stuff went down over the weekend, and so my mind isn't as here as it should be."

The elevator reaches the floor that Owen needs to get off on. Sabrina is going higher, but she makes the choice to get off the elevator with

Leaders are Emotionally Mature, Thoughtful, Smart, Goal-oriented, One-on-one practitioners

Owen in order to finish their conversation. After all, how would it make him feel if she shut him down just after he started opening up?

"I'm very sorry to hear that. How much work do you have on your plate right now?" Sabrina is trying to gauge how detrimental it will be for Owen to miss a couple days of work.

"Well, there's a new training orientation coming up that I need to run tomorrow, which means I really need to be preparing for it today, so. . . ." Owen's voice trails off.

"Okay, okay. Give me just a second to think." Sabrina has learned that if she takes the time and slows down for a moment, she will almost always find a better solution than if she reacts right away.

She starts thinking of the other employees who are capable of running an orientation. Because Sabrina has faithfully held one-on-one meetings with all of them, she knows where they're at and she remembers their preferences. Anna prefers not to run orientations because she experiences anxiety when in front of a lot of people she doesn't know. Edward doesn't mind doing orientations, but he has been known to appear curt with new employees, which can discourage them. Then Sabrina remembers that Nathan has been wanting to prove himself lately, and

Chapter 6: LETS GO!

although he hasn't run an orientation before, he knows how to.

Once she has formulated a plan, Sabrina responds to Owen. "Okay, Owen, here's what I would like to suggest. I don't want you to have to work when you're not able to focus. Family's important, and you should be able to be with them, if that's what you want. So I can have Nathan take over the orientation, and you can take a couple days off work." Sabrina makes sure that she uses language in a way that shows she is merely making a suggestion and trying to help.

"Are you sure?" Owen asks. "I mean, that would be really great."

"Absolutely. I'll go talk to Nathan right now. Just keep me updated, okay?"

"All right. Can do. Thanks, Sabrina. This really means a lot."

When Owen does come back to work, he'll be fully focused on work and he'll remember that Sabrina treated him as a valued employee. The key to success in this situation: Sabrina focused on a win-win option, remembered her employees' preferences, and was able to recall where each of her employees was professionally and emotionally because of frequent and productive one-on-one sessions. She was thoughtful in the way she interacted with Owen

*Leaders are Emotionally Mature, Thoughtful, Smart,
Goal-oriented, One-on-one practitioners*

and emotionally mature in respecting that the individuals in her company had a wealth of things going on in their lives that couldn't always be controlled and that would sometimes get in the way of business. The entire situation makes Sabrina feel good as well; she is truly fulfilled by her role as a leader. Knowing that her employees are doing well helps remind her why she gets out of bed every morning.

But the situation isn't over yet; Sabrina still needs to go speak with Nathan. She approaches Nathan, who is sitting in his office, drinking a cup of tea. He greets her as she enters. Since he is sitting down, Sabrina takes a seat as well to keep the power dynamic even.

"Good morning, Nathan."

"So, what's going on?" he asks, getting straight to the point. Nathan is a very direct person, as reflected by his D and C score in his DiSC profile.

"Well, you remember how you told me that you were interested in working on some training orientations?"

> Recall the "D" and "C" of the **DiSC Profiles:** A "D" or dominance type is one who sees the big picture, is not afraid of being blunt, accepts challenges, gets straight to the point, and places emphasis on accomplishing results. A "C" or conscientious type enjoys independence, employs objective reasoning, wants the details, fears being wrong, and places emphasis on quality, accuracy, and competency.

"Yes."

"An opportunity has come up, and I would like you to run the orientation tomorrow."

"So, I have today to prepare for it?"

"Yes." Sabrina can see that Nathan is a bit skeptical of her suggestion.

"Wouldn't it be better if I had more time to prepare? Perhaps I could run an orientation that occurs later."

"I understand your reservations, Nathan. However, this is as much time as employees are always given to prepare for orientations. I know that you have what it takes to succeed here."

"I'm still not certain."

"How about this? I know Anna doesn't like to run the orientations, but she knows a lot about them and is very good at them. You could ask her for a bit of help. It would be a collaborative effort, at least as far as the preparation goes. Then tomorrow would be your chance to really shine." Sabrina is careful to both encourage Nathan and to make sure that he is equipped to succeed. Sending him in unprepared would be bad for Stuff & Co., Inc., and it would also be bad for Nathan.

"All right, Sabrina. Thank you for having faith in me. I'll try not to let you down!" Nathan commits himself to the task, feeling better because he'll have some help on the preparation.

"I'll check in with you tomorrow, okay?"

Now things really are set up. There's always a chance that Nathan will stumble with the employee orientation, but she knows that he is capable of succeeding.

Sabrina needs to get to her own office now, so she gets back into the elevator and continues taking it up to her floor.

When she reaches her office, Sabrina immediately checks her goal list. She keeps her goal list on her tablet, which is her mobile workstation, and makes sure to look at it every day. It contains day-to-day expectations as well as long-term expectations. It details what she can and needs to do in order to meet her goal. Currently, Sabrina's long-term goal is to increase new employee comfort and happiness because first impressions are lasting impressions. From experience and her own preferences, she knows how important it is to set employees up for success with a welcoming and productive environment, clear expectations, and appropriate resources.

To keep her goals measurable, Sabrina has planned on having new employees start one-on-one sessions as soon as possible, as well as having them complete a quick survey about their

Chapter 6: LETS GO!

first impressions of Stuff & Co., Inc. She looks forward to the opportunity that tomorrow will bring to get her one step closer to that goal. Part of her plan was to more carefully select orientation leaders, which she has already done. Ruling out Anna and Edward as orientation leaders should result in increased employee happiness. She knows that she's taking a bit of a risk on Nathan and knows that Owen has easily proven the most effective orientation leader, but she believes in Nathan's ability. Feeling good about the progress toward her goal, Sabrina continues through her workday as usual.

When the day reaches its end, Sabrina is rather tired—work is a tiring thing no matter how much you love it—and very ready to go home. However, when she's home, she doesn't stop thinking about work. She's driven and committed to being the best leader she can be, and that often means taking a little time to evaluate herself. She thinks that perhaps she could have approached Nathan differently, although she is happy with the result. She is confident in her decision to let Owen take a few days off work. Lastly, she brainstorms about how she can involve herself more with the new employees in order to increase their comfort and happiness.

Leaders are Emotionally Mature, Thoughtful, Smart, Goal-oriented, One-on-one practitioners

A leader's work is never done, and Sabrina keeps challenging herself to be as good a leader as possible, to constantly be emotionally mature, thoughtful, smart, goal-oriented, and a practitioner of one-on-one sessions. Sabrina is in a LETS GO! state of mind that will not only benefit her and Stuff & Co., Inc., it will also help current and future leaders who observe and model themselves on her behavior.

Conclusion

When Justice Sage entered the courtroom five chapters later, all the employees were already seated in the gallery. He was ready to pronounce sentence. "Not guilty," he declared. "Stuff & Co., Inc.'s leaders are in a LETS GO! state of mind."

*L*eaders are *E*motionally Mature, *T*houghtful, *S*mart, *G*oal-oriented, *O*ne-on-one practitioners

For more information or to continue the conversation, please email me at stefanie@letsgolead.com or check out www.letsgolead.com.

www.ingramcontent.com/pod-product-compliance
Lightning Source LLC
Chambersburg PA
CBHW051721170526
45167CD00002B/745